C000000638

AAT

Management Accounting: Costing

Pocket Notes

These Pocket Notes support study for the following AAT qualifications:

AAT Advanced Diploma in Accounting – Level 3

AAT Advanced Certificate in Bookkeeping – Level 3

AAT Advanced Diploma in Accounting at SCQF Level 6

Further Education and Training Certificate: Accounting Technician (Level 4 AATSA)

British library cataloguing-in-publication data

A catalogue record for this book is available from the British Library.

Published by:
Kaplan Publishing UK
Unit 2 The Business Centre
Molly Millars Lane
Wokingham
Berkshire
RG41 2QZ

ISBN 978-1-78415-608-4

© Kaplan Financial Limited, 2016

Printed and bound in Great Britain.

CONTENTS

Preface

These Pocket Notes contain the key points you need to know for the exam, presented in a unique visual way that makes revision easy and effective.

Written by experienced lecturers and authors, these Pocket Notes break down content into manageable chunks to maximise your concentration.

Quality and accuracy are of the utmost importance to us so if you spot an error in any of our products, please send an email to mykaplanreporting@kaplan.com with full details, or follow the link to the feedback form in MyKaplan.

Our Quality Co-ordinator will work with our technical team to verify the error and take action to ensure it is corrected in future editions.

A guide to the assessment

The assessment

MMAC is the management accounting unit on the Advanced Diploma in Accounting qualification.

Examination

Management Accounting: Costing is assessed by means of a computer based assessment. The CBA will last for 2 hours 30 minutes and consist of 10 tasks.

In any one assessment, students may not be assessed on all content, or on the full depth or breadth of a piece of content. The content assessed may change over time to ensure validity of assessment, but all assessment criteria will be tested over time.

Learning outcomes & weighting

1. Understanding the purpose and use of management accounting within an organisation   15%

2. Apply techniques required for dealing with costs   35%

3. Apportion costs according to organisational requirements   19%

4. Analyse and review deviations from budget and report these to management   10%

5. Apply management accounting techniques to support decision making   21%

Total   100%

Pass mark

To pass a unit assessment, students need to achieve a mark of 70% or more.

This unit contributes 20% of the total amount required for the Advanced Diploma in Accounting qualification.

1

Management accounting

- Financial accounting and management accounting.
- The nature of cost accounting.
- Basic terms in cost accounting.

Financial accounting and management accounting

Definition

Financial accounts are an historical record of transactions which are presented in a standard format laid down by law. Such accounts are normally produced once or twice a year and are primarily used by external groups, e.g. shareholders.

Definition

Management accounts can be produced in any format that is useful to an organisation. They tend to be produced more frequently than financial accounts, usually once a month. They contain information required to run a business.

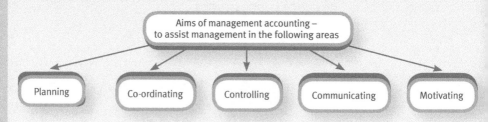

Aims of management accounting – to assist management in the following areas

Planning | Co-ordinating | Controlling | Communicating | Motivating

The nature of cost accounting

Definition

Cost accounting is the process of calculating and recording the costs involved in the production and distribution of products and services.

Main reason for carrying out cost accounting: to calculate the cost of a product and therefore set the sales price of the item.

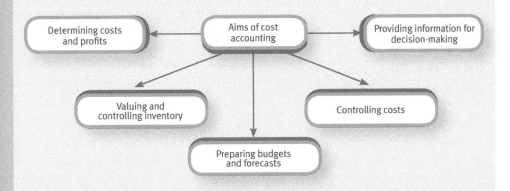

Basic terms in cost accounting

Cost unit refers to the item we are trying to find the cost of. This will normally be the item of a product that an organisation manufactures or a service that an organisation provides.

Examples of cost units

Car manufacturer – car
Paint manufacturer – litre of paint
Accountancy firm – cost per chargeable hour
Hospital – cost per operation

A cost centre is anywhere within an organisation where costs are incurred. A cost centre could therefore be a location, function or item of equipment.

It is important to recognise that cost centre costs are necessary for control purposes, as well as for relating costs to cost units.

There are different types of centres determined by what the manager has control over:

- Cost centre
- Profit centre
- Investment centre

The cost card

A cost card is used to show the breakdown of the costs of producing output based on the classification of each cost.

	£
Direct costs	
Direct materials	250
Direct labour	120
Direct expenses	10
Prime cost (Total of direct costs)	380
Variable production overheads	15
Marginal production cost (total of direct and variable costs)	395
Fixed production overheads	35
Absorption cost (total production cost)	430
Non-production cost	
(e.g. administration overhead; selling overhead)	20
Total cost	450

2

Cost classification

- Cost classification.
- Element and nature.
- Cost behaviour.
- Splitting semi-variable costs.

Cost classification

Cost can be classified as follows:

Classification	Purpose
By element – materials, labour and expenses	Cost control
By function – production (cost of sales), and non-production (distribution costs, administrative expenses).	Financial accounts
By nature – direct and indirect	Cost accounts
By behaviour – fixed, variable, stepped fixed and semi-variable	Budgeting, decision making

Element and nature

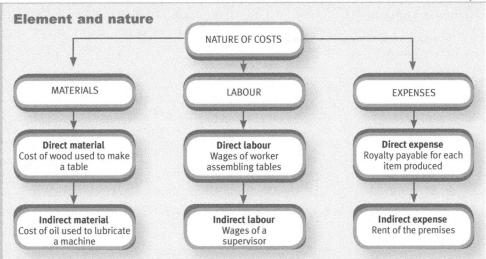

Definition

Direct costs (prime costs) are costs that can be directly related to a cost unit.

Indirect costs (overheads) are costs that cannot be directly related to a cost unit.

Cost behaviour

A **variable cost** increases as the level of activity increases.

A **fixed cost** does not increase as the level of activity increases.

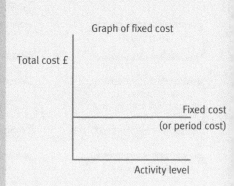

Examples of variable costs:

| Direct materials |
| Direct labour paid using a piece-rate system |

Examples of fixed costs:

| Business rates |
| Management salaries |

A **semi-variable cost** is one that contains both fixed and variable elements.

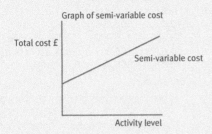

Graph of semi-variable cost

Semi-variable costs are also known as **semi-fixed costs** or **mixed costs**.

Examples of semi-variable costs:

| Electricity costs | – standing charge (fixed) + cost per Kwh used (variable) |
| Salesman's salary – basic (fixed) + bonus (variable) | |

A **stepped cost** is one that remains fixed over a certain range of activity, but increases if activity increases beyond that level.

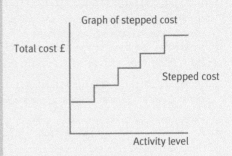

Graph of stepped cost

Examples of stepped costs:

| Inventory storage costs |
| Supervisor salaries |

Splitting semi-variable costs

High-low method

If a semi-variable cost is incurred, it is often necessary to estimate the fixed and variable elements of the cost for the purposes of budgeting. The costs can be split using the high-low Method.

$$\text{Variable cost per unit (VC)} = \frac{\text{Change in total cost}}{\text{Change in level of production}}$$

Fixed cost = Total cost − (VC × units produced)

Example

Production units	Total cost £	
10,000	150,000	
12,000	175,000	Solve using
14,000	195,000	High Low Method
15,000	200,000	

Solution

1 Highest level of production = 15,000 units
(costing £200,000)

Lowest level of production = 10,000 units
(costing £150,000)

2 Variable cost per unit

$$= \frac{\text{Change in total cost}}{\text{Change in level of production}}$$

$$= \frac{£200,000 - £150,000}{15,000 - 10,000} = \frac{£50,000}{5,000}$$

$$= £10$$

3 Substitute in lowest level of production
  Total cost for 10,000 units = £150,000
  = Variable costs of 10,000 units + Fixed costs
  Therefore fixed costs =
  £150,000 − (£10 × 10,000) = £50,000

3

Inventory

- Materials control cycle.
- Materials documentation.
- The stores record card.
- Pricing issues of raw materials.
- Cost of holding inventory.
- Holding costs.
- Systems of inventory control.
- Inventory control levels.
- Integrated bookkeeping – materials.

Materials control cycle

Functions of stores department

Control of purchasing

It is necessary to ensure:

- only necessary items purchased
- orders placed with most appropriate supplier
- goods received match goods ordered
- correct price paid for goods.

Materials documentation

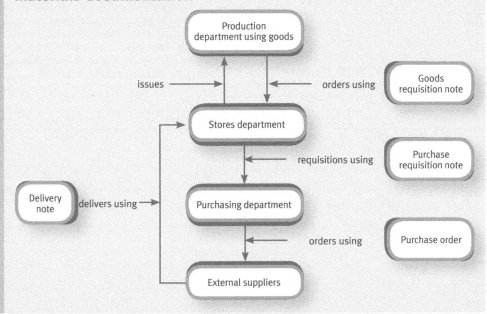

The stores record card

Key Point

When materials are received by stores department, they are checked to ensure correct quantity delivered. The details are then entered onto the stores record card (bin card) which may not have a price column.

Stores ledger account: deals with the accounting of materials (price and quantity) and is maintained by the accounting unit. Physical inventory shown on these accounts is reconciled with the bin card.

Typical stores record card								
Material description :		Component X						
Code	:	X100						
Date	Receipts			Issues			Balance		
	Quantity	Unit price £	Total £	Quantity	Unit price £	Total £	Quantity	Unit price £	Total £

Pricing issues of raw materials

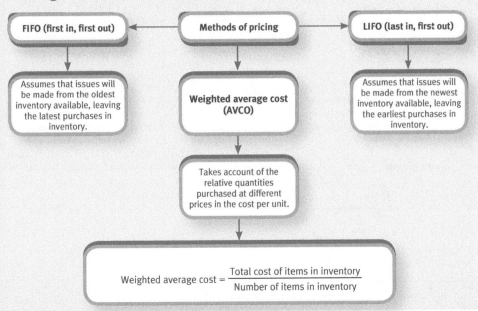

FIFO (first in, first out) ← Methods of pricing → LIFO (last in, first out)

Assumes that issues will be made from the oldest inventory available, leaving the latest purchases in inventory.

Weighted average cost (AVCO)

Assumes that issues will be made from the newest inventory available, leaving the earliest purchases in inventory.

Takes account of the relative quantities purchased at different prices in the cost per unit.

$$\text{Weighted average cost} = \frac{\text{Total cost of items in inventory}}{\text{Number of items in inventory}}$$

Cost of holding inventory

Functions of inventory

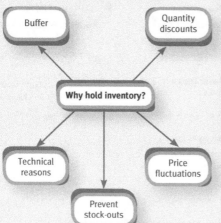

- Buffer
- Quantity discounts
- **Why hold inventory?**
- Technical reasons
- Prevent stock-outs
- Price fluctuations

Inventory control

Definition

Inventory **control**: the method of ensuring that the right quantity of the right quality of the relevant inventory is available at the right time and in the right place.

CBA focus

There are a number of formulae associated with calculating inventory control levels – they are not provided in your assessment and so it is important that you learn them by heart.

Holding costs

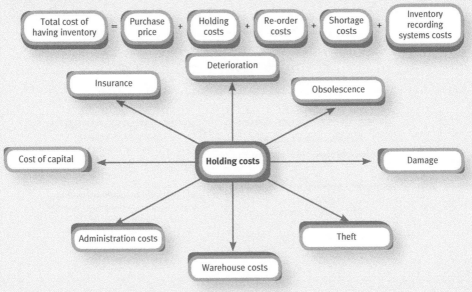

Systems of inventory control

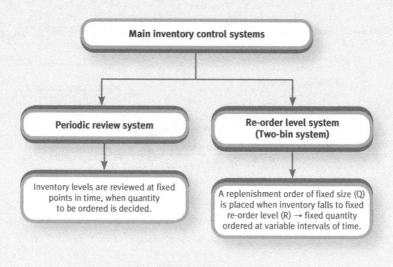

Inventory control levels

Re-order level

Maximum usage × Maximum lead time

Minimum inventory level

Re-order level − (Average usage × Average lead time)

Inventory control levels

$$\sqrt{\dfrac{2 \times Co \times D}{Ch}}$$

Economic order quantity (EOQ)

Re-order level + Re-order quantity − (Minimum usage × Minimum lead time)

Maximum inventory level

Integrated bookkeeping – materials

Materials cost account

	£		£
Opening balance (1)		Issues to production (4)	
Purchases (2)		Returns to suppliers (5)	
Returns to stores (3)		Production overheads (6)	
		Statement of profit or loss (7)	
		Closing balance (8)	
	—		—
	—		—

(1) The opening balance of materials held in stores at the beginning of a period is shown as a debit in the material cost account.

(2) Materials purchased on credit are debited to the material cost account. Materials purchased for cash would also be a debit.

(3) Materials returned to stores cause inventory to increase and so are debited to the material inventory account.

(4) Direct materials used in production are transferred to the production account, which is also known as the Work-In-Progress. The is recorded by crediting the material inventory account.

(5) Materials returned to suppliers cause inventory levels to fall and are therefore 'credited out' of the materials cost account.

(6) Indirect materials are not a direct cost of manufacture and are treated as overheads. They are therefore transferred to the production overhead account by way of a credit to the materials cost account.

(7) Any material write-offs are 'credited out' of the material cost account and transferred to the statement of profit or loss where they are written off.

(8) The balancing figure on the materials cost account is the closing balance of material inventory at the end of a period. It is also the opening balance at the beginning of the next period.

4

Labour

- Employee records.
- Remuneration systems.
- Direct and indirect labour costs.
- Overtime premium.
- Integrated bookkeeping – labour.

Employee records

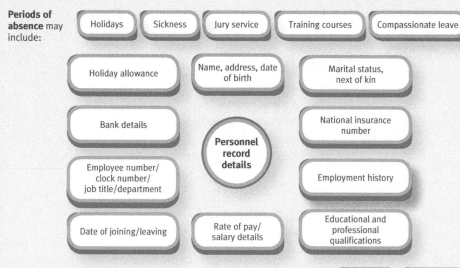

Periods of absence may include:

- Holidays
- Sickness
- Jury service
- Training courses
- Compassionate leave

Personnel record details

- Holiday allowance
- Name, address, date of birth
- Marital status, next of kin
- Bank details
- National insurance number
- Employee number/ clock number/ job title/department
- Employment history
- Date of joining/leaving
- Rate of pay/ salary details
- Educational and professional qualifications

Attendance records show hours worked by employees and are recorded on:

- Clock cards
- Timesheet

Remuneration systems

REMUNERATION SYSTEMS

Annual salaries
tend to be paid to managers and non-production staff

Gross pay (per month)

$$= \frac{\text{Annual salary}}{12}$$

Hourly rates of pay and overtime payments

Mainly apply to production and manual workers.

- Paid for every hour worked.
- Standard hours per week.
- Hours worked in excess of standard = Overtime hours.
- Overtime pay = Basic pay + Overtime premium.

Piecework payments
are made when a fixed constant amount is paid per unit of output.

Disadvantages of this system include no security of income and being penalised for low levels of output which occur for reasons beyond an employee's control (e.g. machine breakdown). To overcome these disadvantages, the straight piecework rate is often accompanied by a **guaranteed minimum payment**.

Direct and indirect labour costs

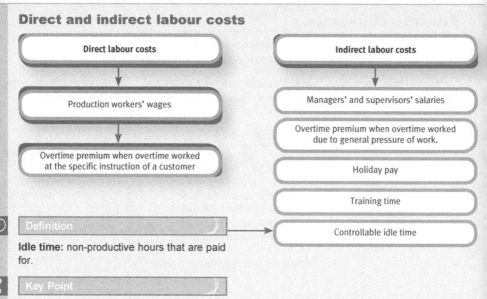

Direct labour costs	Indirect labour costs
Production workers' wages	Managers' and supervisors' salaries
Overtime premium when overtime worked at the specific instruction of a customer	Overtime premium when overtime worked due to general pressure of work.
	Holiday pay
	Training time
	Controllable idle time

Definition

Idle time: non-productive hours that are paid for.

Key Point

The distinction between direct and indirect labour costs is a very important one.

Overtime premium

Definition

Overtime premium is the extra element of payment over and above the basic hourly rate for additional hours worked.

Example

Court works a standard week of 40 hours at an hourly rate of £8.20 per hour. Overtime is paid at time and a half.

Last week Court worked 45 hours.

Gross pay

Basic pay = 40 x £8.20 =	£328.00
Overtime = 5 x (£8.20 x 1.5) =	£61.50
Gross pay	£389.50

Overtime payment

Overtime hours = 45 − 40 =   5 hours

Overtime rate per hour = £8.20 x 1.5 =   £12.30

Overtime payment = 5 hours x £12.30 = £61.50

Overtime premium

Overtime premium is the amount paid over the basic hourly rate for the overtime hours

Overtime premium
per hour = 0.5 x £8.20 = £4.10

Overtime hours = 5

Overtime premium = 5 hours x £4.10 = £20.50

Integrated bookkeeping – labour

Labour cost account

	£		£
Bank (1)	80	Production (2)	60
		Production Overheads (3)	20
	80		80

(1) Labour costs incurred are paid out of the bank before they are analysed further in the labour account.

(2) The majority of the labour costs incurred by a manufacturing organisation are in respect of direct labour costs. Direct labour costs are directly involved in production and are transferred out of the labour account via a credit entry to the production account. The production account can also be referred to as Work in Progress (WIP).

(3) Indirect labour costs include indirect labour (costs of indirect labour workers), overtime premium (unless overtime is worked at the specific request of a customer), shift premium, sick pay and idle time. All of these indirect labour costs are collected in the production overheads account. They are transferred there via a credit entry out of the labour account and then debited in the production overheads account.

5

Expenses

- Direct and indirect expenses.
- Recording expenses.
- Capital and revenue expenditure.

Direct and indirect expenses

Definition

All of the costs incurred by an organisation which are not materials or labour are known as **expenses**.

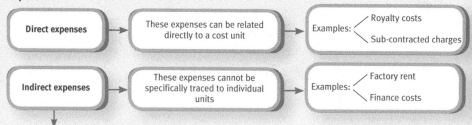

Also known as **overheads**

- **Production overheads** may be accounted for as part of cost of sales (factory rent, insurance, light and heat costs).
- **Non-production overheads** may be accounted for below the gross profit line (administrative costs, selling and distribution costs).
- NOTE: In the real world the term "expenses" could include both direct and indirect components. In the exam, however, expenses are always treated simply as 'overheads' with no separation into direct and indirect elements.

Recording expenses

For control purposes, all costs (including expenses) need to be allocated or apportioned to cost centres and/or cost units.

Direct expenses

Invoices are coded according to the relevant cost unit (product/job/client) before being recorded in the organisation's cost accounting records.

Indirect expenses

Indirect expenses are not directly identifiable with a particular cost unit and are initially charged to an appropriate cost centre.

Allocation

Some expenses will relate solely to one cost centre and will be allocated to the appropriate centre.

Apportionment

Many expenses will relate to more than one cost centre and these costs are **shared** between the appropriate cost centres using a 'fair' basis.
This sharing out is known as **overhead apportionment.**
Overhead apportionment is covered in detail in chapter 7.

Documentation

Most expenses are documented by way of a supplier's invoice or bill. Authorisation and additional information may be attached by way of standard ink stamp with boxes for completion.

Capital and revenue expenditure

Definition

Capital expenditure is expenditure incurred in:

- The acquisition of non-current assets required for use in a business and not for resale.
- The alteration or improvement of non-current assets for the purpose of increasing their revenue-earning capacity.

Accounting treatment

Capital expenditure is initially shown in the statement of financial position as non-current assets. It is then charged to the statement of profit or loss over a number of periods as a depreciation charge.

Definition

Revenue expenditure is expenditure incurred in:

- the acquisition of assets acquired for conversion into cash (goods for resale)
- the manufacturing, selling and distribution of goods and the day-to-day administration of the business
- the maintenance of the revenue-earning capacity of the non-current assets (repairs).

Accounting treatment

Revenue expenditure is generally charged to the statement of profit or loss in the period in which the expenditure was incurred.

6

Basic variances

- Basic variance analysis.

Basic variance analysis

The aim is to be able to compare the costs and revenues of the activity that has actually been completed with what revenue and cost that level of activity should have produced. To be able to make this comparison a flexed budget needs to be produced.

Flexed budgets

A flexed budget calculates the costs and revenues at certain levels of activity based on the budget costs

To be able to produce a flexed budget a good knowledge of cost behaviours is required – see chapter 2.

Overview of cost behaviours:

- Variable – increases in direct proportion with the level of activity and is constant per unit.
- Fixed – remains constant in total at all levels of activity.
- Stepped – remains constant in total to a certain level of activity and then the cost steps up to a new higher constant.
- Semi-variable – there is a fixed element to the cost and a variable element. These costs are separable using the high-low method.

An example of a flexed budget

Units sold and produced	Cost or revenue per unit	1,200	1,800	2,500
	£	£	£	£
Sales Revenue	20	24,000	36,000	50,000
Direct Materials	2.50	3,000	4,500	6,250
Direct Labour	4.70	5,640	8,460	11,750
Variable Overheads	3.50	4,200	6,300	8,750
Fixed cost		6,290	6,290	6,290
Total profit		4,870	10,450	16,960
Profit per unit (2 decimal places)		4.06	5.81	6.78

Variance analysis

Once a flexed budget is produced to match the actual levels of sales and production the costs and revenues are compared.

A favourable variance occurs if the actual revenue received is greater than the flexed revenue or if the actual costs are less than the flexed costs.

An adverse variance occurs if the actual revenue is less than the flexed revenue or if the actual costs are greater than the flexed costs.

An example of a variance statement

	Flexed Budget	Actual	Variance value	Favourable or Adverse	Percentage change %
Volume Sold	1,370	1,370			
	£	£	£		
Sales Revenue	27,400	30,000	2,600	F	9.5
Less costs:					
Direct Materials	3,425	3,875	450	A	13.1
Direct Labour	6,439	6,501	62	A	1.0
Variable overheads	4,795	4,975	180	A	3.8
Fixed cost	6,290	6,300	10	A	0.2
Operating profit	6,451	8,349	1,898	F	

7

Overheads

- Allocation and apportionment of overheads.
- Bases of apportionment.
- Secondary apportionment.
- Methods of reapportionment.
- Absorption of overheads.
- Under/over absorption of overheads.
- Integrated bookkeeping – overheads.
- Absorption costing.
- Activity Based Costing (ABC)

Allocation and apportionment of overheads

Definition

Allocation: charging the whole of an overhead cost to the specific cost centre that incurred it.

Key Point

Overheads arise solely in a particular cost centre. The salary of a supervisor working exclusively in the assembly cost centre would, for example, be treated as an overhead and would be **allocated** to the assembly cost centre.

Definition

Apportionment: the splitting of shared overhead costs between relevant cost centres using an appropriate basis.

Key Point

Overheads may relate to several cost centres – for example, rent, rates and heating costs. Overheads which relate to several cost centres are shared out or **apportioned** between the relevant cost centres on the most appropriate basis.

Bases of apportionment

Type of cost	Basis of apportionment
Maintenance	Number of hours worked/machine time
Insurance of machinery	Carrying amount of machinery
Rent and rates	Floor space occupied (m^2)
Lighting and heating	Volume occupied (m^3)

Arbitrary nature of overhead apportionment

Overhead costs apportioned to different cost centres are simply the result of using a particular basis to share out the overall overheads of a business. If different bases had been chosen then the amounts apportioned to different cost centres would have been different, i.e. the overhead costs are shared out on an arbitrary basis.

Example

Bases of apportionment

SB Ltd has two production departments (Assembly and Finishing) and two service departments (Maintenance and Canteen). The following costs are expected to be incurred.

	£		
Indirect materials	20,000	→	Basis of apportionment = Direct allocation
Rent	15,000	→	Basis of apportionment = Area (m^2)
Electricity	10,000	→	Basis of apportionment = Kw hours consumed
Machine depreciation	5,000	→	Basis of apportionment = Machine value
Building depreciation	10,000	→	Basis of apportionment = Area (m^2)
Indirect labour	55,000	→	Basis of apportionment = Number of staff

The following information is available:

	Assembly	Finishing	Maintenance	Canteen
Area (m^2)	1,000	2,000	500	500
Kw hours consumed	1,000	4,000	Nil	5,000
Machine value	£45,000	£35,000	£11,000	£9,000
Number of staff	20	30	10	–
Indirect materials consumed	£7,000	£8,000	£3,000	£2,000

The information given in this example can be used to calculate the overheads apportioned to the different cost centres. The ways in which this can be done are shown in the next example.

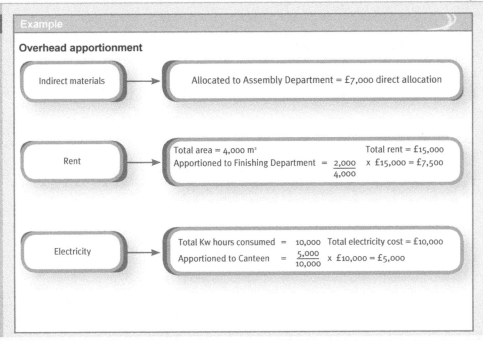

Example

Overhead apportionment

Indirect materials → Allocated to Assembly Department = £7,000 direct allocation

Rent → Total area = 4,000 m²   Total rent = £15,000
Apportioned to Finishing Department = $\frac{2,000}{4,000}$ x £15,000 = £7,500

Electricity → Total Kw hours consumed = 10,000   Total electricity cost = £10,000
Apportioned to Canteen = $\frac{5,000}{10,000}$ x £10,000 = £5,000

Example

Overhead apportionment (continued)

Machine depreciation →

Total machine value = £100,000   Total depreciation = £5,000

Apportioned to Maintenance $= \dfrac{11,000}{100,000} \times £5,000 = £550$

Building depreciation →

Total area = 4,000 m²   Total depreciation = £10,000

Apportioned to Assembly Department $= \dfrac{1,000}{4,000} \times £10,000 = £2,500$

Indirect labour →

Total number of staff = 60   Total indirect labour = £55,000

Apportioned to finishing Dept $= \dfrac{30}{60} \times £55,000 = £27,500$

Secondary apportionment

Reapportionment

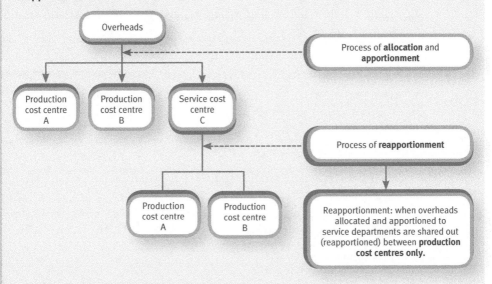

Methods of reapportionment

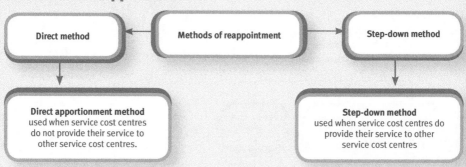

Methods of reappointment

Direct method ← **Methods of reappointment** → **Step-down method**

Direct apportionment method
used when service cost centres
do not provide their service to
other service cost centres.

Step-down method
used when service cost centres do
provide their service to other
service cost centres

 CBA focus

Aims of reapportionment

The reasons for reapportioning service
department overheads is so that all costs are
identified with a production cost centre and
we can then work out the cost of the units
produced by each production cost centre.

It is likely that the exam-based assessment
you will be facing will require you to carry
out a series of overhead allocations and
apportionments.

Absorption of overheads

Absorption rate bases

Having collected all overheads in the production cost centres via overhead allocation, apportionment and reapportionment, the total overhead must be charged to the output of production cost centres. The charging of overhead costs to cost units is called **overhead absorption**.

Various overhead absorption rates exist and the most suitable one should be selected. The use of an absorption rate per unit is for one-product businesses but the following bases may be more appropriate for a multi-product business:

- Absorption rate per direct labour hour
- Absorption rate per direct machine hour.

Direct labour hour rates are commonly used in labour-intensive production whereas direct machine hour rates are commonly used in machine-intensive production.

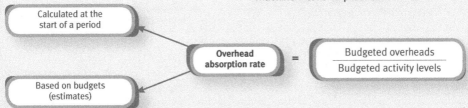

Calculated at the start of a period		
	Overhead absorption rate =	$\dfrac{\text{Budgeted overheads}}{\text{Budgeted activity levels}}$
Based on budgets (estimates)		

Overhead absorption rates

Martin Ltd estimates that the total factory costs for the coming year will be as follows:

	£
Direct materials	40,000
Direct wages	60,000
Prime cost	100,000
Factory overhead	30,000
Total factory cost	130,000

The factory will produce 10,000 units of a variety of different products.

It is anticipated that during the year there will be 30,000 direct labour hours worked and 15,000 machine hours.

$$\text{Rate per unit} = \frac{\text{Budgeted overheads}}{\text{Budgeted production}}$$

$$= \frac{£30,000}{10,000 \text{ units}} = £3 \text{ per unit}$$

Rate per direct labour hour

$$= \frac{\text{Budgeted overheads}}{\text{Budgeted direct labour hours}}$$

$$= \frac{£30,000}{30,000 \text{ hours}} = £1 \text{ per labour hour}$$

Rate per machine hour

$$= \frac{\text{Budgeted overheads}}{\text{Budgeted machine hours}}$$

$$= \frac{£30,000}{15,000 \text{ hours}} = £2 \text{ per machine hour}$$

Under/over absorption of overheads

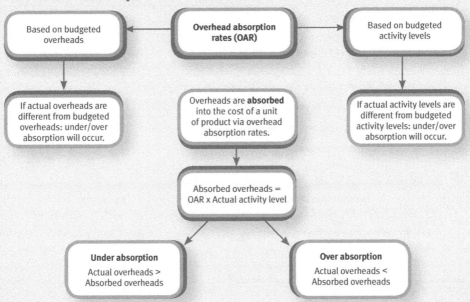

Example

Under/over absorption

A company has a single production department. Its budgeted production overheads for 20X4 were £200,000 and its budgeted volume of production was 50,000 direct labour hours. It has decided to absorb production overheads into product costs on a direct labour hour basis.

During 20X4, actual production overhead expenditure was £195,000.

Calculate the under or over absorption when:

(a) 54,000 direct labour hours are worked.

(b) 46,000 direct labour hours were worked.

$$\text{Overhead absorption rate} = \frac{£200,000}{50,000 \text{ direct labour hours}} = £4 \text{ per hour}$$

(a) Absorbed overhead = 54,000 hours x £4	
= £216,000	£
Actual overheads	195,000
Absorbed overheads	216,000
Over-absorbed overheads	21,000

(b) Absorbed overhead = 46,000 hours x £4	
= £184,000	£
Actual overheads	195,000
Absorbed overheads	184,000
Under-absorbed overheads	11,000

KAPLAN PUBLISHING

Integrated bookkeeping – overheads

Production Overheads

£		£
Actual Overhead cost (1)	Absorbed overheads (2)	
Over-absorbed (3)	Under-absorbed (4)	
———	———	
———	———	

(1) The actual cost of all the indirect costs are recorded as a debit in the production overheads account. The credit is either in the bank or payables account. The actual cost will be made up of all the indirect production costs – material, labour and expenses.

(2) The overheads that are absorbed into production (WIP) are recorded as a credit in the production overhead account. This is calculated as the budgeted OAR x actual activity.

(3) When the account is balanced at the end of the period and the balancing amount is required on the debit side of the account to equal the credit side we have an over-absorption of overheads. The overheads absorbed into production are greater than the actual cost of the overheads. This is recorded as a credit in the costing statement of profit or loss.

(4) When the account is balanced at the end of the period and the balancing amount is required on the credit side of the account to equal the debit side we have an under-absorption of overheads. The overheads absorbed into production are less than the actual cost of the overheads. This is recorded as a debit in the costing statement of profit or loss.

Absorption costing

Absorption costing

↓

Values inventory at full absorption cost of production:
- marginal cost; plus
- fixed production overheads per unit.

↓

May give rise to under or over absorption of fixed overheads

↓

Is a requirement of IAS 2

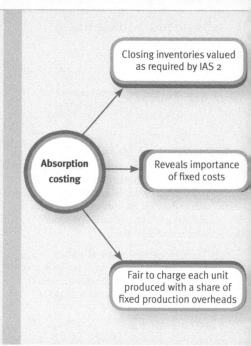

Closing inventories valued as required by IAS 2

Absorption costing

Reveals importance of fixed costs

Fair to charge each unit produced with a share of fixed production overheads

Activity Based Costing

Activity based costing (ABC) is an alternative approach to product costing. It is a form of absorption costing, but, rather than absorbing overheads on a production volume basis it firstly allocates them to cost pools before absorbing them into units using cost drivers.

- A cost pool is an activity that consumes resources and for which overhead costs are identified and allocated. For each cost pool there should be a cost driver.

- A cost driver is a unit of activity that consumes resources. An alternative definition of a cost driver is the factor influencing the level of cost.

Calculating the overhead recovery rate using ABC

There are five basic steps to calculating an activity based cost:

Step 1: Group production overheads into activities, according to how they are driven.

Step 2: Identify cost drivers for each activity, i.e. what causes these activity costs to be incurred.

Step 3: Calculate a cost driver rate for each activity.

Step 4: Absorb the activity costs into the product.

Step 5: Calculate the overhead cost per unit of product

Job, batch and service costing

- Job costing.
- Batch costing.
- Service costing.

Job costing

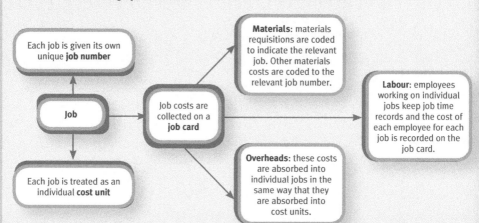

Businesses that use job costing

- Construction companies
- Aeroplane manufacturers
- Vehicle repairers.

Definition

Job costing: the costing system used for a business where production is made up of individual, different, large jobs.

Each job is given its own unique **job number**

Job

Each job is treated as an individual **cost unit**

Job costs are collected on a **job card**

Materials: materials requisitions are coded to indicate the relevant job. Other materials costs are coded to the relevant job number.

Labour: employees working on individual jobs keep job time records and the cost of each employee for each job is recorded on the job card.

Overheads: these costs are absorbed into individual jobs in the same way that they are absorbed into cost units.

Batch costing

Definition

Batch costing: the costing system used for a business where production is made up of different product batches of identical units.

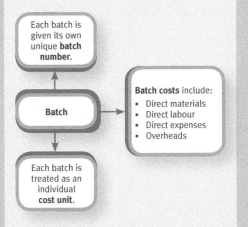

Each batch is given its own unique **batch number.**

Batch

Batch costs include:
- Direct materials
- Direct labour
- Direct expenses
- Overheads

Each batch is treated as an individual **cost unit.**

Example

Batch costing

GA Ltd is a paint manufacturer. 1,000 litres of 'polar white' matt vinyl paint are produced. The production run costs are as follows:

	£
Materials	1,600
Labour (15 hours at £10 per hour)	150

Overheads are absorbed at a rate of £16 per direct labour hour.

Total batch cost	£
Materials	1,600
Labour	150
Overheads (15 hours @ £16)	240
Total batch cost	1,990

Cost per unit for batch

$$\text{Cost per unit} = \frac{\text{Total batch cost}}{\text{Number of units}} = \frac{£1,990}{1,000 \text{ litres}}$$

$$= £1.99 \text{ per litre}$$

Service costing

Definition

Service costing is a form of **continuous operation costing**.

The output from a service industry differs from manufacturing for the following four reasons:

- **Intangibility** – the output is in the form of 'performance' rather than tangible or touchable goods or products

- **Heterogeneity** – the nature and standard of the service will be variable due to the high human input

- **Simultaneous production and consumption** – the service that you require cannot be inspected in advance of receiving it

- **Perishability** – the services that you require cannot be stored

9

Process costing

- Basics of process costing.
- Normal losses and abnormal loss and gains.
- Scrap value.
- Transferring losses and gains.
- Equivalent units and work in progress.
- Treatment of materials and other costs.

Basics of process costing

Process costing is the costing method applicable where goods or services result from a sequence of continuous or repetitive operations or processes.

Examples of industries that use process costing:

- Chemical.
- Cement.
- Oil.
- Paint.
- Textile.

Process costing is very similar to batch costing.

$$\text{Cost per unit} = \frac{\text{Net cost of input}}{\text{Expected output}}$$

Process accounts

In order to keep track of process costs, we prepare a process account for each process. The inputs into the process are debited to the process account and the outputs are credited to the process account.

Process account

	kg	£		kg	£
Materials	2,500	3,500	Output	2,500	4,550
Labour		600			
Overhead		450			
	2,500	4,550		2,500	4,550

Cost per unit =£4,550/2,500kg = £1.82 per kg

Normal losses and abnormal loss and gains

Normal loss

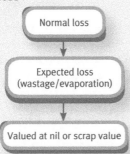

Normal loss

↓

Expected loss (wastage/evaporation)

↓

Valued at nil or scrap value

Normal loss units

1,000 kg or materials were input to a process. Normal loss is expected to be 20% of input.

Normal loss   = 20% x 1,000 kg = 200 kg

Expected output = Input – Normal loss

= 1,000 kg – 200 kg

= 800 kg (80% x 1,000 kg)

Example

Normal loss

1,000 kg of material costing £18 per kg was input to a process in March. Normal loss is 10% of input. Output was 900 kg.

Process account – March

	kg	£		kg	£
Input (1)	1,000	18,000	Output (3)	900	18,000
			Normal loss (2)	100	–
	1,000	18,000		1,000	18,000

Workings

(1) 1,000 kg x £18 per kg = £18,000

(2) Normal loss = 10% x 1,000 kg = 100 kg

Normal loss is valued at zero in this situation.

Workings (continued)
(3) Output = Input – Normal loss
= 1,000 – 100 = 900
Cost per unit

$$= \frac{\text{Total process costs} = \text{£18,000}}{\text{Output} \qquad 900\text{kg}} = \text{£20 per kg}$$

Value of output = 900 kg x £20 = £18,000

Abnormal loss

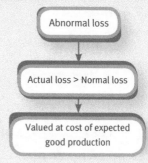

Abnormal loss

Actual loss > Normal loss

Valued at cost of expected good production

Example

Abnormal loss

1,000 kg of material costing £18 per kg was input to a process in April. Normal loss is expected to be 10% of input. Output was 800 kg.

Process account – April

	kg	£		kg	£
Input	1,000	18,000	Output (2)	800	16,000
	1,000	18,000	Normal loss (1)	100	–
			Abnormal		
			loss (3)	100	2,000
				1,000	18,000

Workings

(1) Normal loss = 10% x 1,000 kg = 100 kg
Normal loss is valued at zero in this situation.

(2) Actual output = 800 kg (given)

$$\text{Cost per unit} = \frac{\text{Total process costs}}{\text{Expected output}} = \frac{£18,000}{900 \text{ kg*}} = £20 \text{ per kg}$$

Value of output = 800 kg x £20 = £16,000
*expected good production

(3) Abnormal loss = Actual loss – Normal loss
Actual loss = Input - Output = 1,000 – 800
= 200 kg
Abnormal loss = 200 kg – 100 kg = 100 kg
Abnormal loss value = 100 kg x £20 per kg
= £2,000
Abnormal loss is valued at the same cost as good output, i.e. £20 per kg.

Abnormal gain

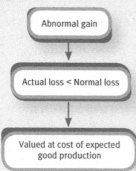

Abnormal gain

↓

Actual loss < Normal loss

↓

Valued at cost of expected good production

Example

Abnormal gain

1,000 kg of material costing £18 per kg was input to a process in May. Normal loss is expected to be 10% of input. Output was 950 kg.

Process account – May					
	kg	£		kg	£
Input	1,000	18,000	Output (3)	950	19,000
Abnormal			Normal loss (1)	100	–
gain (2)	50	1,000			
	1,050	19,000		1,050	19,000

Workings

(1) Normal loss = 100 units valued at zero as before.

(2) Output is valued at $\frac{£18,000}{900}$ = £20 per unit.

Value of output = 950 kg x £20 = £19,000

(3) Abnormal gain = Expected loss – Actual loss

= 100 kg – 50 kg = 50 kg

(Actual loss = 1,000 kg – 950 kg = 50 kg)

Abnormal gain units are valued at the same value as good output, i.e. £20 per unit.

Value of abnormal gain = 50 kg x £20

= £1,000

Scrap value

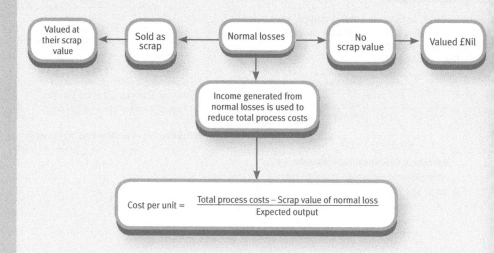

Valued at their scrap value ← Sold as scrap ← Normal losses → No scrap value → Valued £Nil

Normal losses → Income generated from normal losses is used to reduce total process costs

$$\text{Cost per unit} = \frac{\text{Total process costs} - \text{Scrap value of normal loss}}{\text{Expected output}}$$

Example

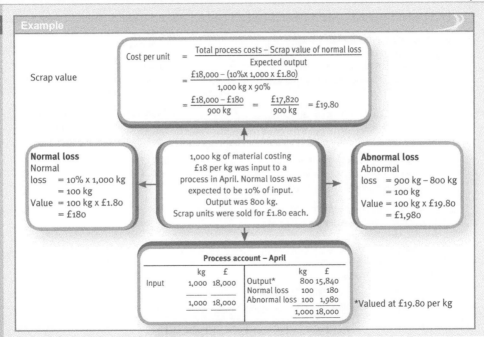

Scrap value

$$\text{Cost per unit} = \frac{\text{Total process costs} - \text{Scrap value of normal loss}}{\text{Expected output}}$$

$$= \frac{£18,000 - (10\% \times 1,000 \times £1.80)}{1,000 \text{ kg} \times 90\%}$$

$$= \frac{£18,000 - £180}{900 \text{ kg}} = \frac{£17,820}{900 \text{ kg}} = £19.80$$

Normal loss
Normal
loss = 10% × 1,000 kg
     = 100 kg
Value = 100 kg × £1.80
      = £180

1,000 kg of material costing £18 per kg was input to a process in April. Normal loss was expected to be 10% of input. Output was 800 kg. Scrap units were sold for £1.80 each.

Abnormal loss
Abnormal
loss = 900 kg – 800 kg
     = 100 kg
Value = 100 kg × £19.80
      = £1,980

Process account – April

	kg	£		kg	£
Input	1,000	18,000	Output*	800	15,840
			Normal loss	100	180
	1,000	18,000	Abnormal loss	100	1,980
				1,000	18,000

*Valued at £19.80 per kg

Transferring losses and gains

Any losses or gains need to be fully accounted for in the accounts of a business. To do this we introduce 2 new accounts – the Scrap account and the Abnormal loss/gain account

To account for the normal loss, abnormal loss or abnormal gain use the following steps:

1. Normal loss is transferred to the Scrap account at the value it is sold at – Cr Process account; Dr Scrap account

2. Abnormal loss or gain is transferred to the Abnormal loss/gain account at the average cost per unit (as per the valuation in the process account) – Abnormal loss: Cr Process account; Dr Abnormal loss/gain account OR Abnormal gain: Dr Process account; Cr Abnormal loss/gain account

3. Abnormal loss or gain is then transferred to the scrap account at the sales value of the normal loss

4. The balancing figure in the Abnormal loss/gain account is the true cost or saving of the loss or gain

5. The balancing figure in the Scrap account is the total amount of cash received from the total loss made.

Abnormal loss example

Process account

	Litres	£			litres	Per unit	£
Material	1,000	30,000		Output	850	42.5	36,125
Conversion		10,000		Normal loss(1)	100	17.5	1,750
				Abnormal loss (2)	50	42.5	2,125
	1,000	40,000			1,000		40,000

Scrap account

	Litres	Per unit	£			litres	Per unit	£
Process account (1)	100	17.5	1,750		Cash (5)	150	17.5	2,625
Abnormal loss (3)	50	17.5	875					
	150		2,625			150		2,625

Abnormal loss/Abnormal gain

	Litres	Per unit	£		litres	Per unit	£
Process account (2)	50	42.5	2,125	Scrap account (3)	50	17.5	875
				SOPL (4)			1,250
	50		2,125		50		2,125

Abnormal gain example

Process account

	Litres	Per unit	£		litres	Per unit	£
Material	1,000		30,000	Output	950	42.5	40,375
Conversion			10,000	Normal loss (1)	100	17.5	1,750
Abnormal gain (2)	50	42.5	2,125				
	1,050		42,125		1,050		42,125

Scrap account

	Litres	Per unit	£		litres	Per unit	£
Process (1)	100	17.5	1,750	Abnormal gain (3)	50	17.5	875
				Cash (5)	50		875
	100		1,750		100		1,750

Abnormal loss/Abnormal gain

	Litres	Per unit	£			litres	Per unit	£
Scrap account (3)	50	17.5	875	Process account (2)		50	42.5	2,125
SOPL (4)			1,250					
	50		2,125			50		2,125

Note

The value of the abnormal gain/loss transferred to the statement of profit or loss

= units × (cost per unit – scrap price per unit)

E.g. Abnormal loss (from above) = 50 × (42.5 – 17.5) = £1,250

Abnormal gain (from above) = 50 × (42.5 – 17.5) = £1,250

Equivalent units and work in progress

Equivalent units (EUs)

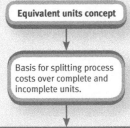

Equivalent units concept

↓

Basis for splitting process costs over complete and incomplete units.

↓

Example – EUs

1,000 units are 50% complete at the end of a period.

EUs = 1,000 x 50% = 500 EUs

Therefore, 1,000 units 50% complete are the same as 500 fully completed units.

Cost per equivalent unit

- Calculated as: $\dfrac{\text{Total cost}}{\text{Number of EUs produced}}$

Summary

- Calculate total EUs.
- Calculate total costs.
- Calculate cost per EU.

Example

EUs and work in progress

In period 1 the following production occurred:
- Started and finished units = 800
- CWIP = 200 units each 35% complete

Costs in period 1 were £11,832.

---

(1) Equivalent units

Units started and finished
800 units x 100% = 800 units

Closing WIP
200 units x 35% = 70 units

Total EUs
800 + 70 = 870 units

---

(2) Cost per EU = $\dfrac{\text{Total cost}}{\text{Number of EUs produced}}$

= $\dfrac{£11,832}{870 \text{ units}}$ = £13.60

Treatment of materials and other costs

Different degrees of completion

Processes usually involve:

- Direct materials
- Direct labour ┐
- Overheads   ┘ → Conversion costs → There may be different amounts of EUs for conversion and materials.

Example

The following data relate to process 1 of a perfume production process.

Volume started in period	3,600 litres
Closing work in process	1,000 litres
Degree of completion of closing WIP:	
Materials	100%
Conversion	65%
Costs incurred in process 1	
Materials	£4,860
Conversion	£7,800

Physical flow of units
Litres started = Litres completed + Closing WIP
3,600 = 2,600 + 1,000

Equivalent units

Input	Equivalent units			Costs	Cost per EU (£)
	Completed in period	c/f in CWIP	Total EU	Total costs (£)	
Materials	2,600	1,000 (100%)	3,600	4,860	1.35
Conversion	2,600	650 (65%)	3,250	7,800	2.40
				12,660	3.75

Opening Work-In-Progress

AVCO	FIFO
• Include the OWIP carry forward cost in the valuation of the cost per EU	• Split the completed units into 'completed OWIP' and those that were worked from 'start to finish'
	• Include the number of EU required to complete the OWIP in the statement
	• OWIP carry forward costs are included at the valuation of output stage.

Example

Reab Ltd makes a product requiring several successive processes. Details of the first process for August are as follows:

Opening WIP:	400 units
Degree of completion:	
Materials (valued at £18,900)	100 %
Conversion (valued at £3,700)	25 %
Units transferred to Process 2	1,700 units
Costs incurred in the period:	
Material	£100,100
Conversion	£86,400

Using AVCO

Equivalent units		Material	Conversion
	Completed Output	1,700	1,700
	Total EU	1,700	1,700
Costs			
	OWIP	18,900	3,700
	Period	100,100	86,400
	Total cost	119,000	90,100
Cost per EU		70	53

Using FIFO

Equivalent units		Material	Conversion
	OWIP to complete	0	300
	Completed Output	1,300	1,300
	Total EU	1,300	1,600
Costs			
	Period	100,100	86,400
	Total cost	100,100	86,400
Cost per EU		77	54

10

Marginal costing

- Marginal costing.
- Marginal versus absorption costing.
- Contribution and profit.

Marginal costing

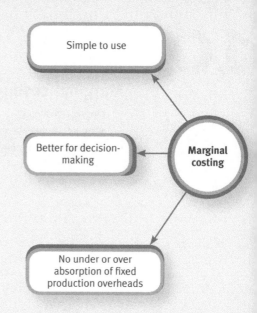

Marginal versus absorption costing

If you are not given opening inventory in a question, assume it equals 0 units.

Key Point

The difference in inventory valuation between marginal and absorption costing gives rise to a difference in reported profits if there is a movement in inventory levels.

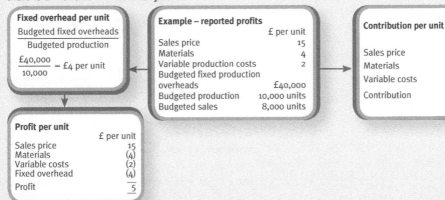

Fixed overhead per unit

$$\frac{\text{Budgeted fixed overheads}}{\text{Budgeted production}}$$

$$\frac{£40,000}{10,000} = £4 \text{ per unit}$$

Example – reported profits

	£ per unit
Sales price	15
Materials	4
Variable production costs	2
Budgeted fixed production overheads	£40,000
Budgeted production	10,000 units
Budgeted sales	8,000 units

Contribution per unit

	£
Sales price	15
Materials	(4)
Variable costs	(2)
Contribution	9

Profit per unit

	£ per unit
Sales price	15
Materials	(4)
Variable costs	(2)
Fixed overhead	(4)
Profit	5

From the example on the previous page, we can calculate marginal and absorption costing profits:

Marginal costing profit

	£
Sales revenue (8,000 x £15)	120,000
Cost of sales (8,000 x £(4 + 2))	(48,000)
Contribution	72,000
Fixed overheads	(40,000)
Marginal costing profit	32,000

Absorption costing profit

	£
Sales revenue (8,000 x £15)	120,000
Cost of sales (8,000 x £(4 + 2 + 4))	(80,000)
Absorption costing profit	40,000

Difference = £8,000

Absorption costing

Only (8,000 x £4) fixed overhead is written off against profit.
Each unit of closing inventory holds £4 fixed production overheads.

2,000 units of closing inventory hold 2,000 x £4 = £8,000 of fixed production overheads

Contribution and profit

Definition

Contribution: the difference between sales price of a unit and the variable costs of making and selling that unit.

Definition

Profit: the difference between total contribution and fixed costs.

Example			Contribution		Profit		

Example

The following data relate to product MWR for a period:

Sales price	£10
Variable costs	£6
Units sold	10,000
Fixed costs	£30,000

Contribution

	£
Sales price	10
Variable costs	(6)
	4

Total contribution (TC)

TC = £4 x 10,000 = £40,000

Profit

Profit	=	Total contribution − Fixed costs
	=	£40,000 − £30,000
	=	£10,000

Remember! There is a direct link between the total contribution and the number of items sold. However, there is no direct link between profit and the number of items sold.

Layout of statement of profit or loss – marginal costing

	£000	£000
Revenue (12,500 x £100)		1,250
Cost of sales		
(at marginal cost, £40)		(500)
Contribution		750
Less: Fixed production costs	400	
Fixed non-production costs	150	
		(550)
Profit for the period		200

Fixed production overheads deducted in total from contribution.

Layout of statement of profit or loss – absorption costing

	£000
Revenue	1,250
Cost of sales (at absorption cost, £72)	(900)
Gross profit	350
Less: Fixed non-production costs	(150)
Profit for the period	200

Fixed production overheads are absorbed into cost of sales.

Cost of sales per unit	£
Marginal cost	40
Fixed cost £400,000/12,500	32
	72

11

Short term decision making

- Relevant costing.
- Cost-Volume-Profit (CVP) analysis.
- Breakeven analysis.
- CVP charts.
- Profit volume (c/s) ratio.
- Assumptions of CVP analysis.
- Limiting factors.

Relevant costing

Any form of decision-making process involves making a choice between two or more alternatives. Decisions will be taken using relevant costs and revenues.

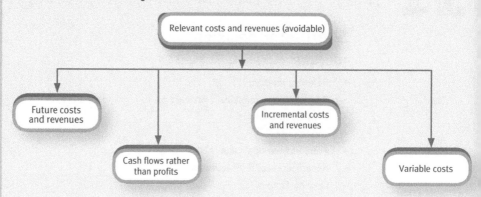

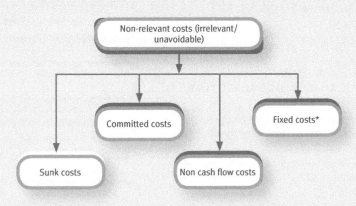

*Note It should be understood that in the long term (by definition) all cost are variable.

Cost-Volume-Profit (CVP) analysis

Definition

Cost-Volume-Profit (CVP) analysis: analysis of the effects of changes of volume on contribution and profit.

Questions answered by CVP analysis:

- How many units do we need to sell to make a profit?
- How much will profit fall by if the price is reduced by £1?
- What will happen to profits if we rent an extra factory and find we can only operate at half capacity?

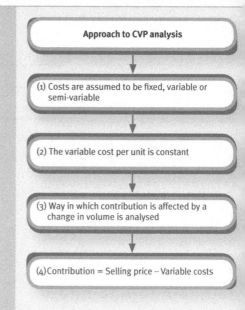

Approach to CVP analysis

(1) Costs are assumed to be fixed, variable or semi-variable

(2) The variable cost per unit is constant

(3) Way in which contribution is affected by a change in volume is analysed

(4) Contribution = Selling price − Variable costs

Breakeven analysis

Breakeven point

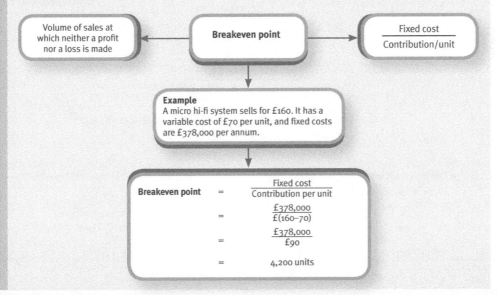

Volume of sales at which neither a profit nor a loss is made

Breakeven point

$$\frac{\text{Fixed cost}}{\text{Contribution/unit}}$$

Example
A micro hi-fi system sells for £160. It has a variable cost of £70 per unit, and fixed costs are £378,000 per annum.

Breakeven point	=	$\dfrac{\text{Fixed cost}}{\text{Contribution per unit}}$
	=	$\dfrac{£378,000}{£(160-70)}$
	=	$\dfrac{£378,000}{£90}$
	=	4,200 units

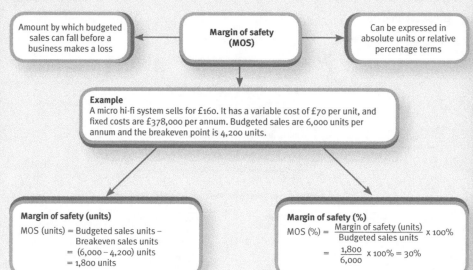

Margin of safety

Amount by which budgeted sales can fall before a business makes a loss ← **Margin of safety (MOS)** → Can be expressed in absolute units or relative percentage terms

Example
A micro hi-fi system sells for £160. It has a variable cost of £70 per unit, and fixed costs are £378,000 per annum. Budgeted sales are 6,000 units per annum and the breakeven point is 4,200 units.

Margin of safety (units)
MOS (units) = Budgeted sales units – Breakeven sales units
= (6,000 – 4,200) units
= 1,800 units

Margin of safety (%)
MOS (%) = $\dfrac{\text{Margin of safety (units)}}{\text{Budgeted sales units}}$ x 100%
= $\dfrac{1,800}{6,000}$ x 100% = 30%

Target profit

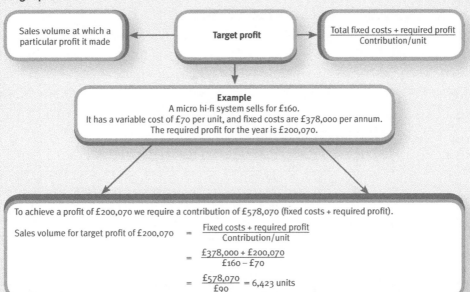

Sales volume at which a particular profit it made

Target profit

$$\frac{\text{Total fixed costs + required profit}}{\text{Contribution/unit}}$$

Example
A micro hi-fi system sells for £160.
It has a variable cost of £70 per unit, and fixed costs are £378,000 per annum.
The required profit for the year is £200,070.

To achieve a profit of £200,070 we require a contribution of £578,070 (fixed costs + required profit).

$$\text{Sales volume for target profit of £200,070} = \frac{\text{Fixed costs + required profit}}{\text{Contribution/unit}}$$

$$= \frac{£378,000 + £200,070}{£160 - £70}$$

$$= \frac{£578,070}{£90} = 6,423 \text{ units}$$

CVP charts

Breakeven chart showing fixed and variable cost lines

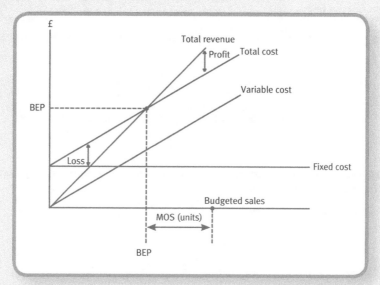

Profit-volume (c/s) chart

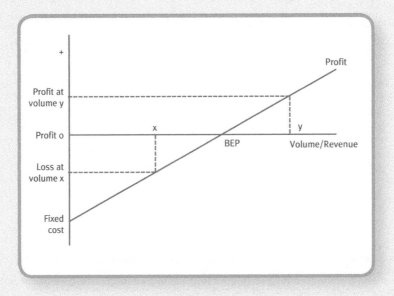

Profit volume (c/s) ratio

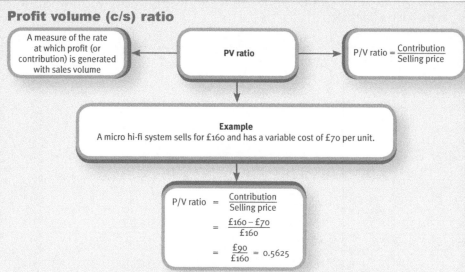

A measure of the rate at which profit (or contribution) is generated with sales volume

PV ratio

$$\text{P/V ratio} = \frac{\text{Contribution}}{\text{Selling price}}$$

Example

A micro hi-fi system sells for £160 and has a variable cost of £70 per unit.

$$
\begin{aligned}
\text{P/V ratio} &= \frac{\text{Contribution}}{\text{Selling price}} \\[2mm]
&= \frac{£160 - £70}{£160} \\[2mm]
&= \frac{£90}{£160} = 0.5625
\end{aligned}
$$

The profit volume ratio is also known as the C/S (contribution/sales) ratio

The profit volume ratio can be used in the BEP and target profit formulae instead of contribution per unit to calculate revenue amounts rather than units.

Assumptions of CVP analysis

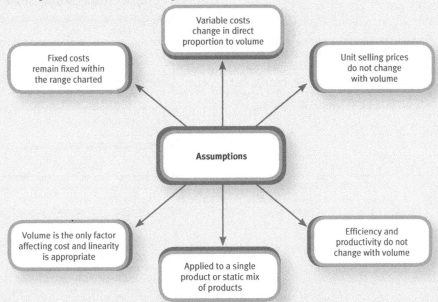

Limiting factors

Definition

Limiting factor analysis is a technique used when we have one resource that is in scarce supply and we can make more than one type of product using that resource. Limiting factor analysis determines how to use this resource in such a way that profits are maximised.

Approach to Limiting factor analysis

↓

(1) Determine the limiting factor that is in scarce supply

↓

(2) Calculate the contribution per unit generated by each product

↓

$$\frac{\text{Contribution per unit}}{\text{Number of units of resource needed}}$$

← (3) Calculate the contribution per unit of scarce resource for each product

↓

(4) Select the product with the highest contribution per unit of scarce resource and make this first

Example

Limiting factor analysis example

Bill makes two products as set out below:

	R	S
	£	£
Selling price	120	50
Material @ £10 per kg	(70)	(25)
	50	25

Bill can sell all the goods he can make, but next year he will be able to purchase only 2,400 kg of material – how should he use this to maximise profits?

	R	S
Contribution per unit	£50	£25
Materials per unit	(£70/£10) 7kg	(£25/£10) 2.5 kg
Contribution per kg	£7.14	£10
Rank	2	1

As S has the higher contribution per unit of scarce resource, Bill should make S.

> **Profits are maximised when contribution is maximised**

Limiting factor analysis with demand constraints

Example

Blake Ltd is subject to a restriction of £6,000 worth of labour hours in one month, which are used to make three products.

	A	B	C
	£	£	£
Selling price	80	20	45
Labour cost	(24)	(6)	(15)
Other variable costs	(20)	(8)	(12)
Contribution	36	6	18

Maximum demand levels in any one month are expected to be 200 units for products A and B and 600 units for C.

Rank products

	A	B	C
Contribution per unit	£36	£6	£18
Labour per unit (£)	£24	£6	£15
Contribution per £ of labour	£1.50	£1.00	£1.20
Rank	1	3	2

Optimal production plan

	Units	Labour £	Contribution £
1 Product A (up to maximum 200)	200	4,800	7,200
2 Product C (£1,200 ÷ £15)	80	1,200 (bal)	1,440
3 Product B	–	–	–
		6,000	8,640

12

Long term decision making

- Payback period.
- Time value of money and discounting.
- Net present value (NPV).
- Internal rate of return (IRR).
- Calculation of the IRR.

Payback period

Definition

Payback period: the amount of time it takes for an investment project to recover the cash cost of the original investment.

CBA focus

Assume cash accrues evenly throughout the year unless told otherwise.

Example

A machine is purchased for £150,000 and is expected to have a useful life of five years. Estimated cash savings over the useful life of the machine are as follows:

Year	£
1	40,000
2	75,000
3	60,000
4	30,000
5	30,000

The payback period for this investment is:

Year	Cash flow	Cumulative cash flow
0	−150,000	−150,000
1	40,000	−110,000
2	75,000	−35,000
3	60,000	25,000

Payback occurs after 2 years and 7 months

Months are calculated 35/60 × 12 = 7

Advantages and disadvantages of payback period

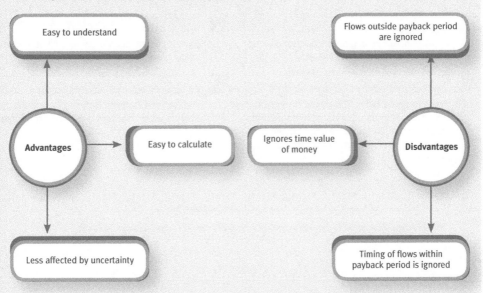

Time value of money and discounting

A key concept in long-term decision-making is that money has a time value.

Definition

Present value (PV): The value at today's date of an amount of cash received/paid at some time in the future, taking account of the compound interest earned over the relevant period.

Only 'relevant' cash flows should be included when assessing a decision.

Definition

Relevant cash flows: Future incremental cash flows that arise if a decision is adopted.

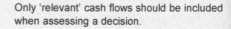

Present value = Future cash flow x Discount factor

Net present value (NPV)

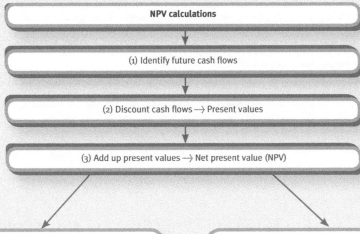

Example

Rug Limited is considering a capital investment in new equipment with estimated cash flows as follows:

Year	0	1	2	3	4	5
Cash flow (£)	(240,000)	80,000	120,000	70,000	40,000	20,000

The company's cost of capital is 9%.

Year	Cash flow £	Discount factor	Present value £
0	(240,000)	1.000	(240,000)
1	80,000	0.917	73,360
2	120,000	0.842	101,040
3	70,000	0.772	54,040
4	40,000	0.708	28,320
5	20,000	0.650	13,000
		Net present value =	29,760

Positive ∴ Accept

Internal rate of return (IRR)

Definition

IRR: the breakeven cost of capital for one investment opportunity. It is the interest rate or discount factor that means that the investment makes no profit or loss i.e. the NPV of the investment = 0

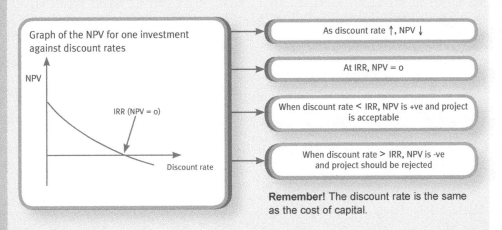

Graph of the NPV for one investment against discount rates

NPV

IRR (NPV = o)

Discount rate

As discount rate ↑, NPV ↓

At IRR, NPV = o

When discount rate < IRR, NPV is +ve and project is acceptable

When discount rate > IRR, NPV is -ve and project should be rejected

Remember! The discount rate is the same as the cost of capital.

Calculation of the IRR

By approximation

The approximate IRR of a project can be estimated by considering how close the NPVs of a project are to zero.

The method used to estimate the IRR is as follows:

- Calculate two NPVs for the investment at different discount rates.
- Estimate the IRR with reference to the NPV values.

If a project has an NPV of £4,400 at 10% and -£31,000 at 20% it can be estimated that the IRR will be closer to 10% than 20% as £4,400 is closer to zero than -£31,000. The IRR will be approximately 11%

By calculation

The IRR of an investment can also be calculated using linear interpolation i.e. it uses two known points on a graph and joins them with a straight line. The point where the line crosses the x-axis will be calculated to provide the IRR.

The method used to calculate the IRR is as follows:

- Calculate two NPVs for the investment at different discount rates
- Use the following formula to find the IRR:

$$IRR\ (\%) = L + \frac{NL}{(NL - NH)} \times (H - L)$$

Where:

L = Lower rate of interest

H = Higher rate of interest

NL = NPV at lower rate of interest

NH = NPV at higher rate of interest

Using the values above:

$$\text{IRR (\%)} = 10 + \frac{4,400}{(4,400 - 31,000)} \times (20 - 10)$$

$$\text{IRR (\%)} = 10 + \frac{4,400}{35,400} \times 10$$

$$\text{IRR (\%)} = 11.24\%$$

Index